DIY SELF-HEALING

USING SRT, THE SUBCONSCIOUS
RELEASE TECHNIQUE

The Newest Tool to Change Your Life Forever

LIAN HENRIKSEN & SHELLY BEST

CONTENTS

FOREWARD

The title of this book was changed from Self-Mastery to DIY Self-Healing as a result of the webinars that were held and because of the change in name, Lian knew a foreword was necessary, she asked the 'Divine' through the 'Osha Zen Tarot Cards' for help and when shuffling, this card just popped out and fell on the table.

Lian took it as a manifestation of what she felt was important to share as the Intention and Foreword for this book. This is the message she was divinely guided to share:

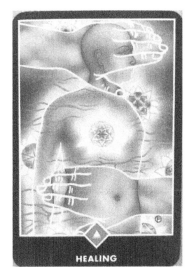

"It is a time when the deeply buried wounds of the past are coming to the surface, ready and available to be healed.

The figure in this card is naked, vulnerable, open to the loving touch of existence. The aura around his body is full of light and the quality of relaxation, caring and love that surrounds him is dissolving his struggle and suffering.

Lotuses of light appear on his physical body, and around the subtle energy bodies, in each of their subtle layers appears a healing crystal or pattern.

When we are under the healing influence of the King of Waters we are no longer hiding from ourselves or others, in this attitude of openness and acceptance we can be healed, and help others to be healthy and whole.

You carry your wound. With the ego your whole being is a wound, and you carry it around.

Nobody is interested in hurting you, nobody is positively waiting to hurt you; everybody is engaged in safeguarding her own wound, who has the energy?.

But still it happens, because we are so ready to be wounded, so ready, just waiting on the brink for anything.

Be aware of your wound, don't help it grow, let it be healed; and it will be healed only when you move to the roots.

The less the head, the more the wound will heal.

Live a headless life, move as a total being and accept things.

Just for twenty-four hours, try it-total acceptance, whatever happens.

Someone insults you, accept it, don't react, and see what happens. Suddenly you feel an energy flowing in you that you have never felt before".

Thank you for picking up this book.

Ask questions, stay curious, you do know the answers, be the light you truly are, so that you help others to recognize the light in themselves. This is true healing.

With Love & Peace,
Lian and Sholly

---◆●---

CHAPTER ONE

Introduction to the Subconscious Release Technique (SRT)

The purpose of this book is to share with you a method that will bring to you a feeling of "instant healing and wellbeing", a process that will quickly and easily bring you to a place of inner calmness, and allow you to move forward from a grounded space of neutrality in any given situation.

The method we will be using is the Subconscious Release Technique (SRT), and in this book we will show you how to use SRT from a self-help perspective.

At the completion of this book you will know how to use SRT to identify your limiting programs and beliefs that are weakening you and by using a kinesiology muscle testing technique combined with a breathing technique be able to release the negative emotions that are trapped within those beliefs and release them at the subconscious level.

The foundation for the SRT program was modelled from a technique called the Bioenergetics Synchronisation Technique, which was a hands on, mind, body and spirit balancing technique created by Dr Sue Morter and practiced by professionals in the health industry to balance the body's energy to reclaim its full potential and heal itself.

The Founder of SRT, Coral Grant developed the program after watching a number of health care professionals using this technique to help people move through some of their biggest limiting programs but, in a new and innovative way, without actually having to touch them.

Coral was not a trained Chiropractor or Massage therapist and so technically was not allowed to touch people however having an innate desire to help people, and a burning question "how can I help people get past their limiting beliefs and programs without having to touch them"?, through Coral's work with Dr Sue Morter, combined with her research and energy work training the Subconscious Release Technique was born.

Coral Grant describes SRT as "a one of a kind energy clearing technique that instantly clears mental and emotional blocks from the subconscious mind and energy field".

In this book you will learn the SRT process that will help you to identify your limiting thoughts, programs and beliefs that are weakening you and triggering stress hormones such as cortisol and epinephrine to be released into your body.

We will show you how to release the negative emotions trapped within those beliefs instantly at the subconscious level, change your DNA, and sever the neural programming so you are no longer able to manifest the same thing again.

Once the emotions have been released, the same event, person or experience that previously would have caused you stress will no longer trigger you, there is a sense of neutrality allowing you to move forward from that neutral space to begin making the changes you desire.

SRT is a calming, non-invasive technique, it requires no machines, drugs or needles of any kind to make the energetic corrections, it simply is an innovative, world class and unique process, a quick and inexpensive tool to create health, wealth and wellbeing in all its forms.

SRT can be used to:

- Achieve goals
- Improve skills

- Eliminate bad habits
- Improve learning ability
- Overcome fears and phobias
- Recover quickly from illness and injury
- Release negative emotions at the subconscious level
- Imprint the subconscious with new and empowering beliefs and programs
- Release self-sabotaging limiting beliefs, programs and patterns at the subconscious level
- Learn to use your own internal bio-computer as an internal lie detector and guidance system

CHAPTER TWO

What is SRT?

The Subconscious Release Technique (SRT) is an effective self-help tool you can use to release beliefs and negative emotions that have been trapped in your body, and in your subconscious usually since you were a very young child.

The source of our beliefs come from our environment, and are influenced by our family, friends, religion, school, geography / location, economic / prosperity, major historical events and media and generally formed by our experiences, inferences and deductions or by accepting what others tell us to be true by a person in a position of authority that you trust and believed, or by emotional impact and are created through repetition.

Most of our core beliefs are formed when we are children with the majority formed within the first 18 years of life and because they are automatic, you don't need to think about them, they are stored at the subconscious level.

The subconscious mind is like the most advanced computer hard drive only more sophisticated and more advanced and estimated to have commenced recording and saving…

- every experience,
- every emotion attached to those experiences,
- our evaluation of those experiences,
- everything we have ever said to ourselves,
- everything we have ever said to others,
- everything that has been said to us,

- everything we think about those experiences, and
- our self image related to those experiences

… since being in the womb.

The Game of Life, by Florence Scovel Shinn says: "Your subconscious is your faithful servant, but you must be careful to give it the right orders, the right words. You have an ever silent listener at your side, your subconscious mind. Every thought, every word is impressed upon your subconscious mind and carried out in amazing detail. It is like a singer making a record on the sensitive disc of the phonographic plate. Every note and tone of the singer's voice is registered. If she coughs or hesitate, it is also registered".

Your subconscious mind is responsible for 95% of your decisions, it controls all your automatic systems, everything you don't need to think about (body functions, breathing, habits), and your conscious mind is responsible for only 5%, making decisions such as what you might like to eat, or drink etc.

Your beliefs are stored in your subconscious and control your automatic behaviours and automatic behavioural responses throughout the day.

For example:

Imagine you're a young child and you come home excitedly to tell your parents about an upcoming school camp, but when you show your parents the form, they take one look at the price, look at you with sadness and say "sorry honey, we can't afford for you to go, I wish money grew on tree's but it doesn't".

In that moment, your heart drops, your excitement dissipates and you are left feeling sadness, disappointment, resentment, anger, guilt and that "there's never enough money around".

In that moment, your subconscious creates the program "there's never enough money around".

You grow up, get a job and have fun spending what you earn, but even when you decide to start saving, you are perplexed as it seems no matter how much money you earn, and how many hours you do, or how many times you do your budget, money goes in one hand and out the other, there's never enough money around, to do what you want.

On many different occasions you find throughout your life, there's never enough money around to do the things you want, and unconsciously find yourself self sabotaging and attracting situations that are in alignment with the belief that you hold creating the reality that makes your beliefs true.

You have thoughts that are attached to those beliefs, and can potentially attach up to 48 different negative emotions and 30 positive emotions to one single thought, and keeping in mind out of up to 90,000 thoughts a day (most unconscious), 70% of them are negative, so your neural pathway of "there's never enough money around" attaches to a plethora of mostly negative emotions creating a neural pathway that gets thicker and thicker throughout your life until you are in a state of utter despair and anxiety around your finances, and you don't know why.

This applies to any area of your life where you are feeling dissatisfied, consciously you know you want better, however if your subconscious has programs that don't support your goals and desires, then you will create experiences that consistently challenge and sabotage your efforts.

SRT disconnects those neural pathways that are holding you back from reaching your goals, dreams and desires through a breathing and muscle testing technique using kinesiology, it removes the negative energy and emotions around your limiting beliefs and programming releasing them at the subconscious level instantly.

When the programming is released at the root cause level it is neutralised at the subconscious level, giving you a clean slate and you get to move towards your goals from a new and empowered state!

CHAPTER THREE

How Does SRT Work?

When we are triggered by our limiting programs, many emotions come into play activating and triggering our Fight – Flight – Freeze response, our system goes haywire releasing cortisol and epinephrine into our body the stress hormones that have the potential to cause us one or more of the following experiences:

-   A faster heart beat
-   Shallow breathing
-   Sweaty palms
-   Frequent visits to the toilet, and
-   Coughing
-   Contraction of the muscles around your heart, shoulders, back and sometimes even the legs

Stress damages the energy powerhouse of our body and can cause or exacerbate many serious health problems including mental health problems such as depression and anxiety, our cardiovascular health such as heart disease, high blood pressure, abnormal heart rhythms and stroke as well as our diet by increasing our cravings for high fat and high sugar foods leading to over eating and causing our body to store fat.

SRT is a breathing and relaxation process that allows your limiting programs and beliefs to be disconnected from the negative emotions that are causing the stress hormones to be released into your body and thereby reducing stress and its associated long term effects.

Through muscle testing we are able to determine which thoughts and beliefs are causing stress to your body, weakening you and taking away your energy and test which emotions are trapped in your system inside those thoughts and programs. We disconnect the neuron in your brain that is connecting the emotions to the belief releasing them it at the root cause level.

The key to releasing the program or limiting belief at the root cause level is to find the very first time you experienced it, and you may be surprised just how easily you will recall an early childhood memory of the first instance, everytime, no matter which program or limiting belief.

The first time it happened, the first time you felt "I am not good enough", "it's too hard", "I can't do this", "how can I compete with him/her, what's the point of even trying", "what if I look stupid", "what if I fail" and felt the cascade of emotions that came with it, the shame, frustration, disappointment, anger, guilt, hurt and unworthiness, your subconscious in its role and function to protect you from that point forward would replay that tape for you.

Times in your life when you considered trying something new, stepping out of your comfort zone and into unfamiliar territory, your subconscious would remind you, warn you even, that debilitating little voice in your head would start, "don't do it, remember it's too hard, remember how you felt, what if you fail, what will people think, better not try at all, than try and fail", throwing everything at you to keep you safe, and in your comfort zone, stagnant, annihilating your courage and motivation and inhibiting your personal growth.

Pandering to your subconscious programming you stay in your comfort zone where it's safe, except your comfort zone isn't even that comfortable, it's familiar but not comfortable, and over time becomes smaller and smaller, and the result is an existence of a life and purpose that is never truly realised.

SRT allows you to move through that programming, and like a dirty windscreen splattered with the 'fears that have been holding you back' clears the screen and wipes them away, erasing old memories and beliefs that no longer serve you and by directly impressing on the subconscious mind new empowering beliefs that do serve you, moves you into a newfound state of peace and empowerment to move you towards your goals.

CHAPTER FOUR

Your Own Personal Inner Guidance System

Dr. Kam Yuen, 35th generation Shaolin Master, specialist in Chinese Energetic Medicine says "The human mind and body functions very much like a modern day computer but our bio-computer is the best computer that will ever be made.

Our bio-computer obeys the same binary principle as the modern day computer. Every conceivable human function can be expressed as "on" or "off", "1" or "0", "negative" or "positive", "strong" or "weak", "Ying" or "Yang", "black or "white.

The binary principle means that there are only two choices to be made on any given condition or situation and in SRT, by the use of a simple muscle response test, the finger and thumb test, you can accurately evaluate what is going on anywhere in the body and mind.

Your personal biocomputer is muscle testing, a method for accessing information in our energy fields, that allows us to determine external influences that weaken or strengthen us using the 'Finger/Thumb Test'.

Using your own finger and thumb to test for responses to your thoughts, beliefs or inquiries and noticing the resistance or lack of resistance in the muscle test, answers are literally at your fingertips.

In SRT, we know that muscles within the body may be weakened or strengthened as a response to thoughts and words, a muscle test can show you which thoughts, words and emotions are creating a weakness in your energy field.

Remember muscle testing is not about a test of will or about physical resistance, it is about accessing information and measuring the response in the change in energy.

You have the ability to be your own detective and weed out thoughts, beliefs and programs that are weakening you. By using this bio-feedback mechanism you have an internal detector that allows you to know what is going on within yourself, where your beliefs support you, and where they don't, without such knowledge we simply are not effectively operating this amazing piece of equipment as the navigation device to success and wellbeing that it potentially is.

This is where SRT has created that bridge, in collaboration with muscle testing creates an operation manual that can guide you through every aspect of life, with time, patience and a gentle persistence, you will soon become an expert operator of your personal biocomputer, and have an inner guidance system that will give you the confidence to change the trajectory of your life.

CHAPTER FIVE

What is a Filler?

Fillers are positive affirmations and beliefs we use to replace old memories, patterns and beliefs and are impressed on the subconscious mind through the conscious mind using the SRT breathing technique.

When choosing new programs to impress upon your subconscious mind for the purpose of moving and accelerating you towards your goals, remember the following:

- Fillers are most effective when practiced over and over and over, even hours at a time, silently or audibly, with quietness but with determination. Imagination and discipline works wonders when practicing SRT and Fillers daily.

- When impressing the subconscious, "active faith" is always necessary ie. you must really believe it will happen, when using the Fillers use your imagination, visualize the end results and really feel the state of freedom it produces.

- Peace and happiness results when all fear is erased from the subconscious, fear is a misdirected energy that can be redirected, or transmuted into faith through consciousness, ie. the moment you become aware of a fear or negative pattern, use the subconscious release technique and Fillers to release and reprogram.

- Remember to use the SRT breathing technique when practicing Fillers, do it as many times as you find necessary, you can use the same filler, or a variety of fillers that resonate and inspire you.

- When working with 'fillers', first acknowledge the problem, turn the problem to your subconscious mind and rest with a deep conviction that once you have released your programs through the SRT process 'IT IS DONE"!

- When using SRT you are in the alpha mind – your conscious mind is submerged allowing affirmations to slip directly into the subconscious for reprogramming.

- You cannot impress your subconscious mind with will power, it is through repetition, faith and expectancy that you reprogram your subconscious mind.

- Sustain your good mood, don't try too hard.

CHAPTER SIX

Applying the Muscle Testing Technique

Let's get you operating your own personal biocomputer so you can begin to navigate and use your own inner guidance system to lead you to the success, goals and dreams you desire.

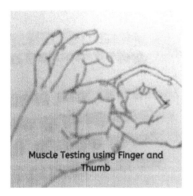

Muscle Testing using Finger and Thumb

Following are the steps to muscle testing using the finger/thumb test:

Begin by making an "O" by joining your left thumb and index finger, then do the same with the right.

Now, interlock the two O's. (see diagram to the left)

Pull your hands away from each other, keeping them closed and **feel the resistance** when you don't want the interlocking O's to pull apart.

Now pull your hands away from each other, and this time **feel the lack of resistance** allowing them to open and release when you want the O's to pull apart.

At this point, you will now have a sense of what the resistance feels like when the 'O' is interlocked and when it is released.

Now can you think about a statement that is true for you while interlocking your fingers in the 'O' position.

"My name is…" (insert your name), or

"I love… " (insert something or someone you genuinely love)

Notice as you make the statement how the resistance level keeps your finger and thumbs closed and locked, this is a *'YES',* a positive response, notice the increase in strength that keeps them closed.

In energy terms, when testing emotions, beliefs or programs this is showing a positive response, that is, the program, emotion or belief strengthens and energises you.

Now think about a statement that is false for you while interlocking your fingers in the 'O' position.

If you are male, say to yourself "I am a female", or

"I hate or dislike…" (insert something or someone you hate or dislike)

Notice as you make the statement the resistance in your fingers and thumbs weaken and they separate and open, this is a *'NO',* a negative response, notice the decrease in the strength that allows them to release and open.

When testing against emotions, beliefs or programs this is showing a negative response which means it is testing weak and requires releasing as it is not a program, emotion or thought that is supporting you.

At first you may find you are not getting accurate responses and will need to educate and train your subconscious mind by doing the following:

- Begin by saying *"YES"* multiple times and holding the connection (interlocked 'O's) firmly.

- Next, say *"NO"*, several times relaxing and letting the fingers (interlocked 'O's) pull apart.

- Let the difference be detectable, but it does not need to be dramatic in degree.

- Continue doing this with questions you know to be genuinely true and false until you are confident the responses are correct.

An affirmative *"YES"* answer always give a strong answer or a closed position, fingers stay closed and interlocked.

A non-affirmative or *"NO"* answer gives a weak response or an opened position, fingers will separate and come apart.

Be patient and practice, remain centered and clear in your mind.

CHAPTER SEVEN

Applying the SRT Process

Dis-ease in the body and mind is simply the subconscious blocking our own natural process and energies to connect with the infinite intelligence within us.

As human beings we live on a variety of levels – physical, mental, emotional, psychological, psychic and spiritual, the physical manifestations of illness and self sabotage that block our success are the result of continued disconnection between and within these levels.

Using SRT, we can learn to locate the exact level, in which the most immediate problem is located, and energetically reverse and remove these negative influences and clear the way for us to begin moving forward towards abundance and prosperity with a clean slate and clear head.

SRT is super easy to learn, super easy to apply on oneself and a simple and unique way to develop your own inner guidance system and healing skills.

You will feel a new level of empowerment and an ability to move through challenges and increase your health, wealth and happiness with ease, flow and grace.

So… let's get started!

First we find your PROGRAMS.

Let's begin by choosing an area of your life that is currently causing you stress, something that is bothering you RIGHT NOW.

Ask yourself this in regards to the area that you are challenged with:

- *"What are your fears"?*
- *"What negative thoughts do you have"?*
- *"What's holding you back"?*

Write your answers down, write freely until you are unable to write anymore, what you're extracting are your limiting thoughts and beliefs, in SRT, we refer to them as programs.

Once you have finished writing, look at each individual program you wrote down, muscle test and notice which programs are weakening you (your fingers will weaken and open).

If the program has no charge, it is not weakening you, your fingers will stay closed and interlocked. If the program is weakening you, your fingers will open and release. Highlight the programs that are weakening you, these are the programs you will clear.

Second we identify and release the EMOTIONS that have attached themselves to your limiting PROGRAMS.

This is where you test which emotions are attached to the program that are weakening you, to do this you will need to refer to the SRT Emotion List provided in Appendix 1.

Lastly we impress upon the subconscious new EMPOWERING PROGRAMS.

The final step is to infuse the subconscious with new empowering suggestions and beliefs, and we do this using "Fillers". You will find a list of empowering "Fillers" in Appendix 2 that you may resonate with and like to use or feel free to create your own.

Let's do a working example together!

A Working Example of the SRT Process

A quick note, the things that you have and love in life, you have because you have a program(s) in your subconscious that supports and allows it, and conversely anything that you struggle with and requires a lot of effort or hard work is because you have programs in your subconscious that don't support you in that area.

Let's look at an example of money.

Five percent of the world's population creates 95% of the worlds' wealth, they have time and money freedom and lots of it, they also have amazing programming around money, for the rest of us, that's 95% of us, a significant portion of the worlds population are left with 5% percent of the wealth, that's a little to share with a lot.

With only 5% of the wealth being shared across 95% of the worlds population it's is easy to imagine that a large portion of us would contain subconscious programming of lack and scarcity.

To give it some perspective, Ladies imagine sharing 95 pairs of shoes between five women, there's a feeling of abundance and prosperity, generosity, sharing and a positive feeling and exchange.

Now imagine having to share 5 pairs of shoes with 95 women, now there's lack and scarcity, a struggle for your piece of the small offering, and with that many women you might not even bother, it's not worth the fight, creating anxiety and potentially a plethora negative emotions.

For the Gents, that's 95 beers between 5 mates, or 5 beers between 95 mates. In the first instance plenty to go around and the second instance, it's up to the strongest or fastest, there's potentially fighting to get in and take a sip and with the competition you might decide why even bother it's not worth the fight.

With a significant portion of people in the world living in scarcity and lack, it's not hard to imagine that a significant portion of us would contain negative programming and beliefs around money.

For example, some common money beliefs you may have heard:

- *"Money is hard to come by"*
- *"Money doesn't grow on trees""*
- *"The rich get rich and the poor get poorer"*
- *"You need money to make money"*
- *"The love of money is the root of all evil"*
- *"People with lots of money are greedy"*
- *"You have to work hard for money"*
- *"Money is dirty, go wash your hands"*
- *"I am always broke", "I never have enough"*
- *"You can't be spiritual and have lots of money"*

The struggle and internal conflict you feel is in trying to override that programming, you're working hard because you want 'something' albeit a goal, money, a relationship and so on, but your undercurrent of belief says "it's not going to happen".

With SRT we get to release that undercurrent!

Ok let's get back to the exercise.

Imagine you have worked through the above exercise and the life area you chose to work on was "MONEY", and when writing down your fears, your thoughts and what was holding you back, one of the programs you wrote down was "I don't have what it takes to be rich".

This program tested weak for you, and now we need to test which emotions are weakening you that are attached to this limiting belief.

You will need to refer to your 'SRT Emotion List' which contains the negative and positive emotions for you to muscle test.

Lets' do this step by step together. First we look at releasing the negative emotions.

Releasing negative emotions

1. Start with the first negative emotion which is 'Aggression'.

    - Recall/think about the program "I don't have what it takes to be rich" and muscle test 'aggression'
    - Notice if your hands remain interlocked or come apart.

2. If your hands, open then the program is weakening you and you need to release the emotion.

    - Take a deep breath, hold your breath and say silently to yourself **
    - *"I release all (aggression) with (I don't have what it takes to be rich)"* and exhale

3. Continue to work through the remaining negative emotions using the same process, releasing all emotions where your fingers release and open.

** Repeat silently to yourself, as you hold your breath this is what activates the subconscious mind.

You will then come to the positive emotions.

Releasing positive emotions

1. When you get to the positive emotions, start with 'Appreciation'.

    -   Recall/think about the program "I don't have what it takes to be rich" and muscle test 'Appreciation'
    -   Notice if your hands remain interlocked or come apart.

2. Where your hands release and open, the program is weakening you and you need to release the emotion.

    -   Take a deep breath, hold your breath and say silently to yourself
    -   *"I release all blocks with (appreciation) with (I am not worthy)"* and exhale **

3. Continue to work through the positive emotions using the same process, releasing all emotions where your fingers released and opened.

Now that we have released the old programming we get to insert some new EMPOWERING PROGRAMS.

Refer to Appendix 2 for a list of empowering "Fillers", choose one or several that you resonate with (examples included below), ***or please feel free to create your own***.

To insert these powerful suggestions at the subconscious level, we will use the same breathing technique to access the subconscious.

1. To impress your subconscious mind you can use one 'Filler' several times, or use several different 'Fillers' that you resonate with.

    Take a deep breath, hold your breath, and say silently to yourself…

    "I am so happy, thankful and grateful I am worthy of abundance in every way, it is my divine right".

    Take a deep breath, hold your breath, and say silently to yourself…

"I am so happy, grateful and thankful that I love money and money loves me".

Take a deep breath, hold your breath, and say silently to yourself...

"I am so happy, grateful and thankful I have a grateful heart that keeps attracting all the things I deeply desire".

To really influence your sense of wellbeing instantly, REPEAT each Filler 3 times!!

CHAPTER EIGHT

Beliefs and the Umbrella Statement Technique – Your Subconscious Hack

When we say we want one thing, but create a vastly different result, that is a clear indication we have an unconscious limiting belief(s) at play, and unless we are willing to bring them into our awareness, identify and change them, those deeply held unconscious beliefs will rule the day.

We understand now that we create beliefs and patterns in childhood that don't serve us in adulthood, much of the meaning we create about the world is based on wrong conclusions, I mean seriously how wise were you at six years old?

Many of our beliefs serve us well until a certain point, however after that some beliefs will become limiting, self-sabotaging and even damaging, for example, if you had an unconscious belief that you don't deserve money, or are unworthy of being loved, or life is a struggle, or there's never enough, or the world isn't a safe place, that is what you will create in the material world.

Consciously you desire the behavior to change, but your unconscious belief(s) become the operating system that determines and influences the choices you make and your results.

The good news is beliefs are highly swappable and when you replace disempowering beliefs with empowering ones, using the SRT Umbrella Statement Technique, tremendous changes can occur in your life at a very rapid pace.

Up to this point, you have learnt the SRT process and how to release the individual emotions attached to your programs and beliefs, however there will be instances where you become aware of a belief, and will not be in a position or have the time to do a deep level clearing, this is where you will use the "Umbrella Statement Technique" instead.

The Umbrella Statement Technique for Rapid State Change

Below you will find a list of some of our most common unconscious limiting beliefs, as you read through them, bring to mind an area of your life where you are challenged, or struggling and as you read through the list notice any that you resonate with.

Breaking through old patterns takes courage, commitment and a willingness to see yourself differently, as you read through the below list, in the area(s) of your life where you have struggled, be willing to take responsibility and confront "what have I been in denial about"?, "what's more important than having what I say I want"?

Highlight any beliefs below that you were drawn to and also notice if it reminded you of similar thoughts or beliefs you have experienced and write them down.

We are going to release the beliefs you identified using the following 'umbrella' statement:

-   *"I release all positive and negative emotional blocks with (insert belief)*

Start with the first belief you identified for example let's use "I am not enough".

-   Take a deep breath, hold your breath and say silently to yourself
-   *"I release all positive and negative emotional blocks with (I am not enough)*

Now that we have released the old belief, let's insert a new empowering belief ie. "what excites you that is completely opposite to the belief you just released"?:

Refer to Table 3 below, or Appendix 2 for a list of empowering "Fillers" or please feel free to create your own.

To impress your subconscious mind you can use one 'Filler' several times, or use several different 'Fillers' that you resonate with.

- Take a deep breath, hold your breath, and say silently to yourself...
- *"I am so happy, grateful and thankful I am enough".*

- Take a deep breath, hold your breath, and say silently to yourself...
- *"I am so happy, grateful and thankful I am perfect as I am".*

- Take a deep breath, hold your breath, and say silently to yourself...
- *"I am so happy, grateful and thankful everything is for my highest good".*

Table 1:

General Universal - Unconscious Self-Sabotaging Negative Beliefs

I am alone… *aka I am on my own*	I am too much	I am not safe
I am wrong… aka I am a mistake	I am crazy	I am not enough
I am not loved	I don't matter	I am not wanted
I am bad… *aka I am evil, I am going to get into trouble, I am selfish, It is my fault, I am a disappointment*	I am worthless… *aka I am not valuable, I am not special, I am disposable*	I am powerless… *aka I'm small and weak, I am not big enough, I am helpless*
I am a failure… *aka I am a mess, I am screwed up*	I am not important… *aka I am not heard*	I don't belong… *aka I am a looser*
I am a burden… *aka I don't need anyone, I am responsible*	I am inferior… *aka I am not as beautiful as, I am not as smart as*	I am not worthy… *aka I don't deserve*
I am different… *aka I am a freak, I am weird*	I am invisible… *aka I am not seen, I don't exist*	I don't have… *aka I am poor, I am deprived*

Table 2: Deep Level - Unconscious Self-Sabotaging Negative Beliefs

Don't talk back to your father/mother	Do it my way
You better show some respect	You had better not make a mistake
I know what is best	You had better not fall
You are just a spoilt brat	You had better be first
Don't be so stupid	Don't rock the boat
You are no good	Play it safe
You don't deserve it	It is us against them
You are the cause of all my problems	You are just like your father/mother
Stop being a nuisance	You will just have to work it out
Pull your socks up	Don't embarrass me
You should have known better	Mind your manners
Don't cause me problems	Silence is golden
I expect better from you	Don't tell the neighbors
You can't remember anything	Keep the family secret in the family
You will always be a failure	Think before you act
Don't be a cry baby	Keep a stiff upper lip
I will give you something to really cry about	Don't upset me or I will get sick
Don't be a smart-alec	Wait until you are my age
You will be the death of me yet	Children should take care of their parents
God will punish you if _____	You will always be my baby
Men are better than women	You will always need me
Women are better than men	Don't have a life of your own
I will disown you if you marry outside our faith	Shame on you
Stay out of my way	How dare you
Leave me alone	Always please others
Women's work is never done	Smile

If it weren't for you, I would be be rich, happy etc	It is hopeless
You have nothing important to say	What is the use?
You have made your bed, now sleep on it	Life is hard
Stay away from Blacks, Jews, Catholics etc	Life is difficult
Why aren't you like…..?	Stop complaining
Be satisfied with what you get	If you think you had it bad, I'll tell you about my life

Table 3: Typical 'LACK' Unconscious Self Sabotaging Beliefs

Money does not grow on trees	Everybody is doing okay but not me
You cannot trust too much	I am alone
You have to work hard to make money	The world is a cruel place
Women need to work harder than men	You are not worthy
You are just a girl	The world is not a safe sapce
The Universe is not a safe place	Life is a struggle
To be of value, you have to be productive	You need to work hard for a living
Who do you think you are?	The rich are bad
I am not good enough	It is a dangerous world
Children are seen, not heard	It is a dog eat dog world
People are mean	There is no single rich men in the city
People are selfish	I am invisible
The world is competitive and scary	life is a test
There is not enough	The job market is so competitive
People are greedy	I must fight with others to get a job
I love to compare myself to others	I have to compete for my share
It is a choice between family and career	Wealthy people are mean
There is no utopi	Women have long hair but little brains.
You are born a sinner	Clients have limited funds

Fillers – Empowering Beliefs

There is always support from the Universe	I am enough
It is safe to let go	It is an abundant Universe
Everything is an opportunity	We are all source energy
There is always support	I am perfect as I am
I am whole and complete	There are no mistakes

The Universe is always working in my favour	Everything is for my highest good
We are equal to all and lesser than no one	Everything is an opportunity
There is always harmony- it is the ebb and flow of the Universe	There is always more out there
There are tons of people out there and there is a perfect one for me	We have so much love around us because the Universe is made up of love
There are always friends and family to support me	There is more fish in the sea than you can catch

CHAPTER NINE

How to Access Your Magic Space Within

A Simple Exercise to Connect with the Magic Space within using the SRT Umbrella Clearing

The objective of this daily routine is to connect with your magic space within, the space in which your light is, the space where your divine seed resides, the space through which you are connected with the Divine, Infinite Wisdom, Oneness, Infinite Consciousness, God, or Tao... the name is immaterial.

This concept of the Divine is extremely useful *"unable to perceive the shape of you, I find you all around me, your presence fills my eyes with love, it humbles me you are everywhere".*

The SRT Umbrella Releasing Technique is invaluable done on a daily basis, and where possible best done just after you get up.

Make this your daily routine, and a deep sense of peace and well-being will flood into you:

- Take a deep breath, hold your breath and say silently to yourself...
- *"I release all positive and negative emotional blocks with what would it take to be with my magic space"* and exhale **
- Repeat this a minimum of 3 times

Impress upon your subconscious using the following Fillers:

- Take a deep breath, hold your breath and say silently to yourself...
- I am so happy, grateful and thankful that I am using the next 15 minutes to nurture myself.
- I am so happy, grateful and thankful that I am connecting with the Divine within
- I am so happy, grateful and thankful that I am giving myself, healing and love

Stay still and continue breathing deeply in, notice the pause and breath out, you will reset any urges to sleep or any sleepiness that may arise.

This is simply your old subconscious programs rising up and wishing to stall or stop the process you are undergoing to awaken your divine self.

The more you go into this Magic Space within yourself, the more you will experience 'the magic', it is here you will be shown:

- Your ideal new habits
- Your life choices
- New perspective on subjects that were previously emotionally difficult for you
- What to eat
- Where to go, who to be with and to learn from
- All these answers will help you to bloom as YOURSELF, as your Soul would like
- You will be "shown" your divine tasks, which will bring a richness and fulfillment to your life that you have never known before
- You will be rewarded with new situations and interactions.
- There will be changes, even if it is prioritising in a way you have never done before
- And, there will be a step in faith as you step into the unknown

You can even ask questions like:

- Who am I?
- What am I doing?
- How will I survive?
- What is my true nature?
- Am I being just self-important?
- Do I know what it means to love myself?
- Why must I act in faith and trust the Divine in me?
- What changes do I need to make?
- What new character qualities must I develop and integrate?
- What wisdom did I learn from past experiences?
- What wisdom did gain from past unpleasant experiences?
- What is my life style living my full potential?
- What is my role in the Global Reorganization?
- What are the blocks that stops me from stepping into the role.

Remember the Purpose of being on Earth is to know your essence, to know your light that is within.

Your heart desires joy, freedom and play. You heart is built for JOY. All   joy needs are opportunities to arise.

Ask yourself on a daily basis, "what are the conditions that most consistently yield joy in my life?".

It is the greatest gift to bring joy into the heart of others, lightening them from their pre-occupation and density of the energetic-thought patterning of the separate self (self-importance). *Joy* interrupts and lifts you out of the mind set of self-importance!

Ralph Waldo Emerson, an American essayist, lecturer, philosopher, and poet who led the transcendentalist movement of the mid-19th century captures it beautifully when he said *"The purpose of life is not to be happy (happiness as we are made to know it!). It is to be useful, to be honorable, to be compassionate, to have made some difference, you have lived and lived well".*

PART 2

CLEARING FOR HEALTH, WEALTH AND INNER HARMONY

CHAPTER TEN

SRT Clearing for Health – The Corona Virus

The Corona Virus has triggered all forms of fear. There are so many stories, did it come from a monkey in China, or is it human created in connection with the 5G.

We see stock markets falling, property prices falling, and in many countries the property market at a complete standstill.

Our TV's are full of news of large international companies firing employees because of falling sales, smaller companies having to close and hundreds of thousands of people are out of a job.

Airlines have reduced their flights, international trains and buses are almost at a standstill, borders closed and country after country in lockdown, and all this caused by the apparent need for social distancing.

Everyone has their opinions, but the important question is "How does all this make you feel"?

Are you watching and taking in the news without question? Are you being absorbed into the negativity? Has this made you question or become aware of how easily you can be or are being influenced by the opinion and point of view of others?

What is most important for your level of wellbeing is "How are you reacting and how are you responding"?

You be wondering is it even possible to rise above this sea of chaos and maintain peace within ourselves, feel in control despite the drama playing out in the world around us?

We are all so unique and perceive things in different ways, however we will always go one of two ways, we can see ourselves as victims, helpless and suspicious or we can be neutral, thereby freeing ourselves from judgement and aggressive energy that we too often direct at ourselves and others.

If we can remember that everything is energy, and that the vibrational frequency of fear, confusion and judgement is low as well as all virus types including the corona virus, then a great strategy to adopt to avoid falling ill is to choose to remain in high vibrational frequency and neutrality is high vibration, and the SRT process releases negative emotions and programs thereby creating neutrality.

So let's get clearing!!

Following are some of the most common thoughts and programs we have uncovered in coaching sessions with Clients triggering fears and feelings of confusion and hopelessness.

Previously we have taught you the deep level clearing, where you find the program and go through the extensive list of emotions to ensure you release at a deep level. But, sometimes you won't be in a position or have the time to clear on that level.

In that case you can use the "Umbrella Subconscious Release" technique, which allows you to clear on the move and at any time of the day!

Test which of the below programs are weakening you and highlight the programs that test weak.

"Why are things changing so unpredictably"

- *"Did the virus come from China"*
- *"How is 5G going to affect me"*
- *"Am I under surveillance"*
- *"Will I be considered weird if I can remain calm and peaceful in this situation"*
- *"Will I be considered irresponsible if I take a drive in my car"*
- *"What if I fall ill and nobody knows"*
- *"What if my family gets it"*
- *"Am I irresponsible if I go out for a walk for fresh air"*
- *"Why can't the scientists find a vaccine soon"*
- *"I hope we go back to normal soon"*
- *"What if I get it"?*
- *"I must be strong"*

Notice if any of your own unique programs are triggered as you read through this list and add any of your own.

Take a deep breath, hold your breath and say silently to yourself:

"I release all positive and negative emotional blocks with (insert program)" and   exhale
Continue releasing all programs that tested weak.

OR, if you feel as though you need to do a deep level clearing on any of the programs, then refer to your SRT Emotion list, and muscle test the emotions with each program as per below:

"I release all (negative emotion) with (insert program)" and exhale.
"I release all emotional blocks with (positive emotions) with (insert program) and exhale.

After you have used the Umbrella SRT technique, or the deep level clearing technique, refer to Attachment 2 and choose one or several empowering NEW

Fillers to reprogram your subconscious.

For example:

Take a deep breath, hold your breath, and say silently to yourself...

"I am so happy, thankful and grateful that every day, in every way I am a prosperous, creative and innovative being".

Take a deep breath, hold your breath, and say silently to yourself...

"I am so happy, grateful and thankful for the confidence, excitement and joy that awaits me".

Take a deep breath, hold your breath, and say silently to yourself...

"I am so happy, grateful and thankful that I get to create my own reality".

To really influence your sense of wellbeing instantly, **repeat** each Filler 3 times!!

CHAPTER ELEVEN

SRT Clearing for Wealth

Another major block for a large proportion of the population is our fear of running out of money. It's a viscous cycle where we are often left feeling vulnerable, powerless and miserable, and not surprisingly a silent thief of our mojo and our motivation that can be sufficient enough to destroy our chances of achievement in any undertaking.

Our current climate is triggering a lot of fear in this aspect of living, the fear of poverty, but how would you know if you were already living with this underlying fear sabotaging your success?

Signs that you may be experiencing this underlying program may include some or all of the following:

- Fear of poverty
- The paralyses of the faculty of reason
- Your imagination is all but destroyed
- Self doubt, and a lack of confidence in self-reliance
- Undermining of your enthusiasm
- Discouragement of your initiative
- Uncertainty of purpose
- Lack of enthusiasm
- Increase in procrastination
- Diminishing self-control

You may have also experienced some or all of the following mindsets:

Expecting poverty instead of demanding riches – overtime you forget you were born to be great, it's in our DNA, we are meant to be rich.

Indifference – this is commonly expressed through a lack of ambition, a willingness to tolerate poverty and an acceptance of whatever compensation life may offer you without protesting, there is a lack of initiative, imagination, enthusiasm, self control as well as mental and physical laziness.

Indecision – the habit of permitting others to do your thinking, staying on the fence.

Doubt – generally expressed as reasons or excuses to explain and justify one's failure(s), sometimes shown in the form of envy of those who are successful by criticising them.

Worry – usually represented by finding fault with another, scowling and frowning, nervousness, self- conscious and lack of self- reliance.

This one area alone can have a dramatic impact on our mental and spiritual health, deciding that nothing which life has to offer is worth the price of worrying creates poise, peace of mind and a calmness of thought resulting in an overall sense of wellbeing and happiness.

Over-caution – the habit of looking for the negative side of every circumstance, thinking and talking of possible failures instead of concentrating upon the means of succeeding. Knowing all the roads to disaster but never searching for the plans to avoid failure and always waiting for the right time.

Procrastination- the habit of putting off until tomorrow that would have been done last year.

These fears are inherent in all of us and depending on our life and experience are internalized to varying levels of detriment and self sabotage, with SRT we can release these programs and the emotions attached to them that are releasing stress hormones into our body and weakening us, clearing out the old energy so we may focus on the next inspired action we need to take towards our goals and desires.

So… let's get clearing!

Test which of the below programs are weakening you and highlight the programs that test weak.

- *"My tendency of 'making do' and compromising"*
- *"My indecision on which path to take, money-wise"*
- *"My indifference with money"*
- *"My doubt on earning as much money as I can earn"*
- *"My worrying over money, both receiving and giving"*
- *"My over caution with spending"*
- *"The way I procrastinate"*
- *"How I am always asking everybody I know, what to do with my money and time"*
- *"How I don't listen to myself"*
- *"Not trusting myself with money"*

Notice if any of your own unique programs are triggered as you read through this list and add any of your own.

With the programs that tested weak (your fingers release and open) take a deep breath, hold your breath and say silently to yourself:

"I release all positive and negative emotional blocks with (insert program)" and   exhale.
Continue releasing all programs that tested weak.

OR, if you feel as though you need to do a deep level clearing on any of the programs, then refer to your SRT Emotion list, and muscle test the emotions with each program as per below:

"I release all (negative emotion) with (insert program)" and exhale *"I release all emotional blocks with (positive emotions) with (insert program)*

After you have used the Umbrella SRT technique, or the deep level clearing technique, refer to Attachment 2 for one or multiple empowering NEW Fillers to reprogram your subconscious.

Take a deep breath, hold your breath, and say silently to yourself…

"I am so happy, thankful and grateful I always have more than enough of everything I need

Take a deep breath, hold your breath, and say silently to yourself…

"I am so happy, grateful and thankful for the excellent and positive things that continue to happen in my life".

Take a deep breath, hold your breath, and say silently to yourself…

"I am so happy, grateful and thankful I spend money under direct inspiration, wisely and cheerfully knowing my supply is endless".

Take a deep breath, hold your breath, and say silently to yourself…

"I am so happy, grateful and thankful I am moving in the right direction".

Take a deep breath, hold your breath, and say silently to yourself…

"I am so happy, grateful and thankful for my attitude of accepting and embracing whatever comes my way".

To really influence your sense of wellbeing instantly**, *repeat*** each Filler 3 times!!

CHAPTER TWELVE

Energy and Inner Harmony

The world we live in is comprised of energy, everything is energy. Nikola Tesla, Scientist & Engineer 1856-1943, said "If we want to understand the Universe think in terms of Energy, Frequency and Vibration." All the experiences we have are the result of how we process the energy of our thoughts.

As humans, we perceive things on basically 3 levels, 3 different densities, the 3rd, the 4th and the 5th.

The 3rd density is the way we observe the world based on Newtonian Physics, everything is solid, everything is real, everything is cause and effect. This is where our victim mentality resides, we feel we are helpless, victims of the events happening around us, powerless with no control or influence over those events or our experience of it. This is our ego consciousness, also known as fear-based consciousness.

When we move into the 4th density, we move into the higher state of consciousness, we are starting to let things be, we understand that we are energetic beings, that we are conscious beings and we have the ability to rise above all drama that is going on around us.

In the 4th density we no longer associate deep value to physical things such as money, status, positions and power. We allow those things to just be, yet we are still identifying and still judging the 3rd density event(s). We have learnt to process things in our own lives at the 4th density, but as we are spiritual beings having a human experience we will still switch back to judgement of the world in the 3rd density.

When we move into the 5th density, we start to understand, live and experience the world as just a holographic experience, where nothing is real. The world is not a hard and challenging place unless we choose it to be. Existing from this higher sense of being, energy, frequency and vibration we are able to rise above the drama and detach from the drama playing out around us.

When we are in this place, and even when challenged by people and events, we will be free of the melodramatic thoughts that create fear and anger and instead of "oh my God what am I going to do?" and the tendency to retaliate and want to protect oneself, we can take action not out of fear, but consciously decide to come from the heart where true empowerment lies.

What has this got to do with the corona virus? When we live in a world where everything is energy, and like energy attracts like energy, that means if you perceive an issue as fearful, and make it real, that is what you are going to experience.

What we get to choose to do is keep ourselves, our thoughts, and our emotions at a high frequency of energy and rise above the situation, and the panic.

This may sound esoteric but it is backed up by quantum science. The most important thing we can do for our health and wellbeing is to stay in the high frequency of love, acceptance and forgiveness, at every moment viewing the world through love, loving energy is 1,000 times more powerful than negative energy.

All viruses are low frequency energy and is why some people get sick while others don't, it all comes back to their own personal frequency level, when you keep yourself at a high frequency, guess what, viruses of low frequency simply cannot attach to you, because your frequencies don't match!

APPENDIX 1 SRT EMOTION LIST

SRT (Subconscious Release Technique) Statements:
I release all (Negative Emotion) with (Program).
I release all blocks with (Positive Emotion) with (Program).

SRT Emotion List

Aggression	Rage	Knowledge
Anger	Resentment	Letting Go
Annoyance	Resistance	Love
Anxiety	Revenge	Memory
Apathy	Rigidness	Nourishment
Boredom	Sadness	Open
Confusion	Shame	Organization
Contempt	Skepticism	Peace
Cynicism	Sorrow	Receiving
Despondency	Stress	Safe
Disbelief	Stubbornness	Support
Disappointment	Terror	Surety
Discontent	Uncertainty	Thankfulness
Doubt	Worry	Trust
Dread		
Embarrassment		
Envy	Appreciation	
Evil	Belief	
Fear	Calm	
Frustration	Certainty	
Grief	Compassion	
Guilt	Creativity	
Hate	Enjoyment	
Hopelessness	Faith	
Humiliation	Feeling	
Hurt	Fulfillment	
Irritation	Giving	
Jealousy	Gratitude	
Judgement	Happiness	
Nervousness	Harmony	
Overwhelm	Honesty	
Pain	Hope	
Pressure	Kindness	
Punishment	Knowingness	

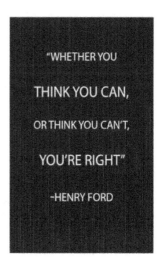

"WHETHER YOU

THINK YOU CAN,

OR THINK YOU CAN'T,

YOU'RE RIGHT"

-HENRY FORD

APPENDIX 2 FILLERS

Use the SRT breathing technique when practicing any of the below affirmations that resonate with you.

** H,T&G – happy, thankful and grateful

- I am so HT&G I am open to receiving more than I can imagine, love, abundance and support
- I am so HT&G I have a grateful heart that keeps attracting all the things I deeply desire
- I am so HT&G I am safe
- I am so HT&G I am happy
- I am so HT&G I am powerful
- I am so HT&G I am unstoppable
- I am so HT&G I am free
- I am so HT&G I am open
- I am so HT&G I am blessed
- I am so HT&G I am a blessing
- I am so HT&G that I am creative
- I am so HT&G I am receiving better than I can imagine, in all areas of my life
- I am so HT&G for the wealth that keeps coming into my life
- I am so HT&G that every day I am becoming wealthier and wealthier
- I am so HT&G I own more wealth than I ever imagined
- I am so HT&G I feel happy and fulfilled in providing for my loved ones
- I am so HT&G that I have more than enough of everything that I need
- I am so HT&G for this magnificent flow of great and inexhaustible abundance in all areas of my life
- I am so HT&G I am extremely prosperous

- I am so HT&G that abundance and prosperity is attracted to me, and I am attracted to them
- I am so HT&G because good and positive things continue to happen in my life
- I am so HT&G that every day, in every way, I am getting better and better as a human being
- I am so HT&G I have a grateful heart that keeps attracting all the things that I deeply desire
- I am so HT&G I know I deserve to be prosperous in everything I do
- I am so HT&G for every good thing that comes to me as a blessing from the universe
- I am so HT&G that the world is a wonderful place to be in and I enjoy my journey on earth
- I am so HT&G I am surrounded by love and joy everywhere I go
- I am so HT&G I am a prosperous, creative and innovative being
- I am so HT&G I am eliminating all the bad habits from my life and creating new positive ones
- I am so HT&G I start every day by feeling deep gratitude for the excitement and joy that awaits me
- I am so HT&G I have everything I want, I am loved, I am loveable and I love everyone
- I am so HT&G money comes to me in increasing qualities on a continual basis from multiple sources
- I am so HT&G my actions create constant wealth, prosperity and abundance
- I am so HT&G for my wealth mind set
- I am so HT&G I always have more than enough money.
- I am so HT&G for everything I receive
- I am so HT&G I release every block that holds me back from receiving
- I am so HT&G that wealth flows to me from all directions
- I am so HT&G to be drenched with financial abundance and I

generously share my wealth.

- I am so HT&G my riches are forever increasing as I give more of myself in service to the world
- I am so HT&G that I love money and money loves me
- I am so HT&G that I am an attractive and irresistible magnet for money
- I am so HT&G money is simply an energy that allows me freedom
- I am so HT&G money loves to be around me and multiply
- I am so HT&G money loves to be around me and is my obedient servant
- I am so HT&G I can and will pursue all of my dreams
- I am so HT&G I have a wonderful business in a wonderful way, and give wonderful service for wonderful pay
-

Two BONUS Affirmations referenced from Dr. Joseph Murphy for creating Wealth

Attract Money

Commentary: The urge of the life principles in you is towards growth, expansion, and life more abundant. You are not here to live in a hovel, dress in rags, and go hungry. You should be happy, prosperous and successful. Never criticize money or those who have plenty of it. Cleanse your mind of all weird and superstitious beliefs about money. Do not ever regard money as evil or filthy. If you do, you cause it to take wings and fly away from you. You lose what you condemn. You cannot attract what you criticize.

Affirmation: I like money, I love it, I use it wisely, constructively, and judiciously. Money is constantly circulating in my life. I release it with joy, and it returns to me multiplied in a wonderful way. It is good and very good. Money flow to me in avalanches of abundance. I use it for good only and I am grateful for my good and for the riches of my mind

Secure a Constant supply of Money

Commentary: recognizing the powers of your subconscious mind and the creative power of your thought or mental image is the way to opulence, freedom and constant supply. Accept the abundant life in your own mind. Your mental acceptance and expectancy of wealth has its own mathematics and mechanics of expression. As you enter into the attitude of opulence, all things necessary for the abundant life will come to pass. Let this be your daily affirmation; write it in your heart.

Affirmation: I am one with the infinite riches of my subconscious mind. It is my right to be rich, happy and successful. Money flows to me freely, copiously and endlessly. I am forever conscious of my true worth. I give of my talents freely and I am wonderfully blessed financially. It is wonderful.

THE AUTHORS' PERSONAL TESTIMONY

Shelly Best

How Shelly came across SRT and became a co-creator of writing this book, was through her desire to create an incredible life not just for herself and her family, but through her passion for helping others to live a life of health, wealth, freedom and abundance.

Even as a young girl, growing up in a single parent family as the oldest of 4 kids, Shelly intrinsically knew life was meant to be fun, full of opportunity and abundance, and tired of the lack and the struggle she vowed to figure out how.

What she discovered was that when you don't have the success you desire, there is something that you don't yet know, you have not yet grown to the level of the person you need to become to have the life, the results, the success and the money you truly desire.

You had to be willing to develop, to work, to stretch, to do that one thing you feared the most, step outside your comfort zone, take inspired action and grow.

When you are willing to do that, to always be looking for opportunities to become the best version you can become, you will find yourself in the right place, at the right time, connecting with the right people which at first appears a random occurrence, to soon thereafter being recongnised as a serendipitous moment manifested from your greatest inner desires that changes the trajectory of your life and sets you on the path to reaching the goals and dreams you were destined to achieve.

After one half hour SRT session with Lian, the sabotaging patterns Shelly was able to instantly release that had plagued her adulthood were so deep and profound, she knew this was a life changing technique that was her destiny to share with others.

In only a few more sessions Shelly was able to heal her marriage that was a heartbeat away from divorce, release deep seated, unresolved patterns from her childhood around wealth, manifest her dream home right next to the beach, and embody a newfound sense of confidence, clarity, vision and motivation that was instrumental in propelling her life, business and relationships.

Shelly is an NLP Master Practitioner Life Coach who has passionately devoured the personal development world for over 20 years on a quest to understand what makes us tick and what keeps us stuck and with that understanding find the best tools available to master your state and wellbeing, your life and destiny and create a life of freedom and abundance that every human being on this planet deserves, SRT is one of the sharpest tools you can carry in your toolkit to create a masterful life.

SRT is such a simple process, so easy to learn, and so easy to use and it is Shelly's hope that the techniques in this book will help you to find and release those patterns that no longer serve you and empower you to fulfil your dreams and create the success, freedom and abundance you are destined to achieve.

Lian Henriksen

Lian was first introduced to SRT when she was being challenged by all the different software programs she needed to learn and navigate to succeed in her group coaching business, painstakingly Lian's learning was slow going.

After working with an SRT Mind and Energy Coach Expert Lian found herself buzzing through tech tools like a rocket scientist, video editing and filming, holding online meetings, creating eBooks and online courses, where previously her flight, fight, freeze response would be instantly triggered, causing her a great amount of stress that kept me stuck her stuck and unable to move forward.

Since learning SRT clearing and releasing techniques, Lian has experienced more joy and optimism, reaching a higher vibration which allowed her to trust simply by being more relaxed in her body.

Lian discovered a newfound sense of confidence that released her from taking other people's words and remarks so personally, and accepting people for who they are.

Most impressively, SRT energetically cleared a program where Lian would look to men for validation and unable to say "No" to their financial pleas for help, had left her close to financial ruin, clearing a major block to her path of true freedom.

For the last 6 years, Lian has been helping young professional women learn self-love and self-mastery through inner child work and guided alpha-mind meditations. With a background in teaching the Law of Attraction and performing as a Reiki Master Teacher, Lian has been able to incorporate these elements with SRT and create major impacts in my clients' lives.

Her qualifications and why should you listen to her:

- SRT Mind & Energy Coach 2019,
- Reiki and Schiem Master Teacher of the Dr.Mikao Usui lineage 2018.
- Law of Attraction Coach from QSCA, USA 2013.
- Trained Acupressurist, The Department of Traditional Medicine, Hanoi Medical College, Vietnam.
- Ayuverdic Yoga Massage trained by Sidhamo Micheal Johnson.
- Hoffman Process – Inner Child 1998

- Certified Healer trained by Charlotte Pedersen of the Bob Moore lineage.
- Businesswoman – Owner Director of Kiki Design AS (closed in 2003).
- Bachelor of Business Studies, London (1967)

For more info, visit us at:

Store

https://singleandsavvymoms.com/collections/clearing-of-general-negative-limiting-subconscious-programs

YouTube

https://www.youtube.com/channel/UCI5-K0_oRTZq2RMb0WQpL_g?view_as=subscriber

Website

https://www.lianhenriksen.com/

Made in the USA
Monee, IL
12 May 2021